[
ariadne/
dark
dark
shine
]

PELEKINESIS
112 Harvard Avenue, #65
Claremont, CA 91711
WWW.PELEKINESIS.COM

ISBN: 978-1-938349-78-2
eISBN: 978-1-938349-81-2
Library of Congress Control Number: 2017957284

Beasley-Baker, Caroline
[Ariadne/Dark Dark Shine]

Book Design, Layout, & Photos by C. Beasley-Baker
www.cbeasley-baker.com

[
ariadne/
dark
dark
shine
]

poems by

CAROLINE BEASLEY-BAKER

Pelekinesis

for my dad, Wilbur J.

Where Squirrels play — and Berries die
And Hemlocks — bow — to God.
EMILY DICKINSON/*#475*

. . .

and I thought love would always be
that brilliant on the wing and wild.
IBYKOS/*LAST SUN IN THE TREETOPS,* 6TH C. B.C.E.

in memory of

HOLLY ANDERSON

1955 – 2017

Signal back — if anyone can, it's you.

poems & mesostics

poems & mesostics

photos

31E studio with viola assist

starlings in american elm/1

preamble/labyrinth (or circle?)

lost/found/&-repeat.
the arcing thread —
a whip/lifeline/way/
          the-magical-gift-given/odd-bit —
discovered in an old sewing basket.
[who sews nowadays?]
no enchanted sword or mirror —
how much braver to pocket the spool of thread —
head out — put your finger to a pulse and count.
a puzzle sometimes —
which simple thing reveals a boon.

dowsing/we find our way in 5 colors (odysseus)

. . . so from water does the soul.
HERACLITUS/FRAGMENT #68

she says:
the sea/the sea —
my truest ocean crowned

Regina-
the-iodined-Pacific-Blue —
no other salted water smells so life enthralling.

he says:
the pond/the pond —
a tablespoon of my bone chips still inhabits

the water verge
where minnows spawn —
&/waterflow reflects the sun/a Pale Pellucid Gold.

(yet/in his absent heart the reef off isla santa barbara waits.)

she could say:
the lake/the lake — the young man/
his step dad/drifting in a small wooden boat —

drinking beer/catching catfish in the
Haunt Black ozark shadows.

the contented/lucent child-
who-sits-between-
them — kaleidoscopes
Gold Violet in the dip of sun.

(yet/she's seen too many waterbodies made waste&spoil.)

he could say:
take me home to salty water.

&/so — she will.
this Ruby-colored water glass turns water into
wine or whatever one might wish:

your finest streaming ocean/endless salty reach.

bell/a ring grows around rosie-o

whosoever is desired
is most surely
lost

in the interregnum of
the in between — o-where-o
of the fixity of past/flux of memory.

bereft
amidst bijou/
the chiming chatter

— ruddy
hem-hem-
atite — retracting stars/a
willow. the belted kingfisher
clatters

(water/grass)
in exult of bird bones/n'salty rime —
this regnal auroral . . .

(amidst
chiming chatter
the chittering chimes
clamor — after all what
matters?)

the toll
for thee — knell/
the chiming chatter.

flowers/mudhra/seine (loose pearls)

1914/a few heartbeats before the war in 5 colors

paris.
ahhh Icterine —
the warbling breast
of one small/
sorrowless bird:
il passe/il passe.
& i recall
Jet Black silhouettes/
cut-paper trees —
our gaiety — us
improvising:
love-along-the-seine.
& skywriting —
your warm breath
in the chill Moon Glow/
Midnight Blue:
il passe/il passe.
so tenderly — you
take my hand.
i hear birdsong turns
Melodious
the further south we go:
il passe/toutes les passe.
you take my hand.

the **L**ength of

y**O**ur

fi**N**gers

a**G**ainst

m**I**ne —

expecta**N**t /

Grateful.

certitude/a thing so rare in 5 colors

i see
my first singleton
starling in a parking lot:

so sparkling/
so many speckled-colors —
Green/Yellow/Blue/Brown Black/
    & shimmery —

the most beautiful bird!
that is — until
the flock lands.

(a startle of starlings — really?!)

the multitude/
a Dullish Black
diminished in an instant —

peck/pecking for any crumbs.

they of course
don't care what i am/
what i think:

what of my way too common eyes?
what of my desire to abjure the ordinary?

another-redux/not quite spring in 4 colors

i sit
on my bed
looking out my window
upon the shades
of brick —
Classic Brick/Char/& Brown Gray —
on this Frail Blue day . . .

i watch the twining of the not-yet-
resurgent-wisteria into the branches
of *my-paramour/*
    my-bare-American-Elm . . .

i sit
in this old brick house/
i sit
on a ball in space
in the deep obliteration/
the end times of this one cold season.
the winter seems
to say:

je suis désolé —
i know the coming of the forsythia/
the concupiscence of the lily.

wisteria on gray stucco wall

concupiscence/wisteria & elm

the early sun has risen.
the world out there
is battling into spring —
all set to run amok —
with Cupid's essence
stirring-
in-the-stems/the-shoots-
&-branches.
the tree/the vine:
the trailing
entwine of one —
the dominion of
the other — the two of them
annex — each-to-next.
they rope-in-shadows/re-
calibrate/describe . . .
the birds/squirrels —
the bees —
are they ornaments
only?
& me?

[✳] :
we elide the past.
we belie the existence of oblivion.
we breach gravity&separation.
we know nothing of your notion 'to-conquer.'

iF

I

tRy now

to seE

our First kiss —

i see Lights

— brIef /

greEn /

So bright.

inception/confection (valentine)

ba-baby/baby —
baking you a cake
as fast as i can!

a ca-catastrophic event —
late heavy ba-bomb-
ardment/
hail of meteorites —
kablams of such ferocity . . .
oceans boil-off into incandescent mist
while you hiss/percolate/
cool.

you perfection — singular pearl —
be mine.

memento/honoring the sweet dead

a strange day —
engaged in an email wake
for an old high school friend
who has just died of complications
from diabetes.
am astonished at the different lives/
all of the sentiment
— i'd forgotten
fond remembrance
is a balm — go figure.
i may just end up
with a few conservative friends:
we know difference doesn't preclude
affection . . .
it also makes me see
i felt alienated pretty early on.
so — after all —
am drinking a nice glass
of some good French sparkling
to the in-general-locus-of-life
to my now-gone-friend — aka
Meathead to his young self's chagrin
and to the chagrin of the boys/
now men who had named him so . . .
yet
an interesting thing re these men —
they seem to have been better

friends — boy to boy —
than i knew —
knowing them and not.
am sure they
were muddled back then
but somehow they had pledged
themselves to one another so simply —
you can still hear it in their words —
the tenderness.
they are certainly more sentimental
than the women who seem
more circumspect —
less wedded to the past
less caught up in medieval romance.
but then the girls' experience
was more circumscribed:
he dated both me and my sister —
a gentleman always. sympathy/
kindness — our laughter . . .
however it is —
am trying to sort this beyond
clichés — boys-stage-center —
& find then/now —
thankfully — whether
X-chrome or Y- —

it's reassuring to know a kind soul
is recognized — there is grace in this.
so my dear friend(s):
*salut/salud/chin-chin/l'chaim
et alia — to life!*

american elm/snow

daily-life/drifting in Deep White to no purpose in 2 colors

i'd
say what
saves us is
remove — the bobsled's Blue-
steel-

flashing-runners against the Blue snow

as
we slip
into the — fall-
out — bunkered-blindness: deracinated-
sublimity

revolving sweetness . . .

yet —
the afterbirth
is troublesome — & what
to do when no-horses-no-king's-men:
no-queen&women-to-put-it-together-again —
      bruise/the-broken-crown/the-

all-fall-down?

bound&delivered/are you listening in 4 colors

after Damien Echols, writing from Death Row —
incarcerated at 20, released on new evidence having
served 18 years, 78 days.

[killer/killed/the falsely blamed — the bereaved
(all of us) each lamb/wolf goes to slaughter?
the 'guilty' not-guilty in this instance
but guilty or not what virtue
in death as punishment —
momentary thrill/a sense of justified?
is justice served or lost?
there is no revival —
gone is gone — state
murder to punish murder makes
murderers of us all — a fact.
& in murdering do we not murder ourselves
one soul at a time?
it's not in some divinity's eyes
but mine that worries me here.
let's stop the killing —
think again.
there must be a better way.]

i've been pushed
i've pushed myself as far as i can go —

a cliff edge — running on
pain/on paranoia&contempt.

[on:
fear/the Pitchest Black —
fury/this Ravaged Red —
hatred/an Excoriating White
           Rose . . .
— the light here is Shit Brown and medieval].

& please —
Do You Hear Me?
me screaming so loud
the   wind   is   blowing   through   your   hair.

*italics show a paraphrase of Damien Echols' words.

sLay

hIm —

Kill

thE

nAive

fooL.

he speAks of

Miracles —

Blunders

into Love

wIthout

Knowing — he

disbelievEs in

Sweet
innoce**N**ce
with**O**ut
Wiles.

blushed rose (just becuz)

to-quote/anonymous (∞)

[*
because π
is a transcendental
number —
squaring the circle
is not possible
in
a finite
number of steps
using
the classical tools —
the compass&straightedge.]

& the rose?

shadow-play/to cease to be in 2 colors

set/reset:
the flame gutters
goes up in smoke
what else could I expect?
. . .
the flame gutters —
the candle wick
is burned
down to near zero —
its heat is mirage:
its spirit —
refulgent/
turning in on itself —
goes-up-in-smoke.
in the hesitation that follows the first
moment of absence
i think —
it must be magic/a hat trick —
what else could i expect?
(all dying does this to me.)
i
hold onto the after-
glow of that which is gone.
but since i'm not particularly holy —
a ghost
in the mind's
eye

is merely Ephemera:
mysterious/Bittersweet —
a fleeing comfort
in the sure presence of past.
this is not to deny remembrance —
a prime # of self — or
the possibility of *forever-
after-life* — (metaphysical
so why not) —
but more to say/as always
my true vocation is in living/
in the anodyne of —
simple things.

night/the back gardens

doleful/even if the sky is Blue in 1 color

S.A.D.
& genes
& the fucking
world same-as-it-
ever-was
(surely
while glorious/
happily mundane too/& —
right?)
sorry . . .
the bottom
of the canyon/quarry/lava-hole/whatever
is where we start
to look up again —
right?

(a
spent leaf coolly spins
past my window: lyrical/
lazy/complete.)

errant/by any other in 3 colors

he
calls his boat —
my-righteous/beauteous-

Rose —
after me.
he sails this boat —

secure in wood —
downriver —
beyond calm water

past harbor into tumult: the-burning-

reverie . . .
a-floating-stick/flame-on-water —
until — at long last —

he
settles upon
a safe shore in comfort.

he jokingly
calls the place —
thank-god-the-land-Forget-Me-Not

— &
names his clapboard house
Celestine-the-sky/

she-who-once-was-the-sea.

blue bowl of red roses

*you*R

*ch*A*rms*

D*iminish*

H*eaven* —

i A*m*

W*eak* —

*tak*E *my*

*h*E*art* —

P*ity my*

*de*S*pair.*

to-steal/thou shalt or not in 1 color

she
was in kindergarten
when she claimed
another
kid's painting as her own
— the-most-perfect-Orange-
          pumpkin
she'd ever seen.
it
was easy —
the teacher said:
who painted this pumpkin?
&
no-doubt-about-it
she raised her hand . . .

what
she couldn't calculate
then but/what
sub-
sequently came to be
is that several times over in her
life —
the fruits of her
hands/her labor were stolen.
karma after all?

each of us
caught up in the cycle of to-
        do-unto/have-done-to-you
until conscience/entropy reigns —
the weight/measure of the deed undoes?

american elm/early spring

vivify/lift me up in 4 colors

[❄]
Gray/White/Black —
a few stars?
from the far back of the cave —
the hush/hush of the
still-torporing she
bear:
it's
about time
my lazarusa —
see the Pale-ish-Blue . . .

| ❋ >:
is the world spring-like/sprung?
are you curious? do you rise to
shine — in thrall to need/
to waking be?

afloat/adventures on the high sea (the new world)

[late morning]

a
slow track
of sugar ants dis-
placed — the vacuum bag's
ant farm:

purgatory? obfuscated grace?

[late afternoon]

a-
kimbo in
the rocking boat
on the lookout for the dis-
appearing/marauder bladderwort —

so goes the water flea . . .

[blood moon/full lunar eclipse]

absconding
a wild turkey 3-some high steps
along the saltwater marsh-
      edge

gobble-
a-gob-gobbling
agreeably about nothing
much: bounteousness?

[daybreak]

/\/\/\/
together we measure each wave crest to trough.

will in the world with rat/i-pad on stripes

blue-b**L**ack

misch**I**ef-maker/

Thief — now

you **T**rem-

b**L**e.

th**E**

dar**K**

River

b**I**rds

hu**S**h —

t**H**e moon is

tangled i**N** her

h**A**ir.

archaeologic/rains it pours in 2 colors

dreary out —
& i'm thinking of writing
a note to a friend —
something formal on Ivory-
colored notepaper — an
anachronism:
    let me
lasso you back/
eclipse the void moon/
align the stars with vega —
if i can. if not/
then at least —
    let me
sift the loess/upgrade
you to luxury class
this next time around.
    truly —
no effort too great.
or would you prefer —
something less showy — a
Gold-thimbleful of my heart-
felt admiration
for all that is fine in you?

topsy-turvy/thru the wormhole in 1 color

flopsy/mopsy
have gone before —
cottontail/he minds the store . . . .
& another alice
meets the young will shakespeare (!)
en passant. he's
sporting
Bleach White/tooled
& top-stitched leather gloves —
ornate/seriffed text
spools from off the tip of
his waggling/
his songbird's tongue . . .
& —
to die/to sleep/to dream?

tell us — the seraphim say
— *is that fire eating the open door?*

breach/Black ice in 1 color

abyss
of almost —
the end-will-be —
that/which consumes us
daily without
our
ever/even looking
up until aiyeeeeeeeeeee
we're
flat up/gobsmacked
against it — a
terrifying
kind of blessing.
nothing to
do
but be thankful/
alive. &
to
say '*here . . .*'
to the rest-of-us:
night terrors/blind
wanderings/the reaching out —
(i perseverate & pray) —
all those things
most of us do when faced
with the truth of almost-forever-gone.

here
we are —
slip/slidin' away:
willing flight/the next
cold breeze.

crosswalk/late night

boat**S**

on w**A**ter —

n**I**ghts

ree**L**ing

am**O**ng

the sta**R**s.

doe**S**

thi**S**

m**A**ke

h**I**m

comp**L**ete

or d**O**es she

still hau**N**t him?

idle-thought/Gray day in 1 color

dwindle/dwindle —
i split in two/un-
    do/un-
        spindle:
i disassemble
unseen or attended to —
a-concatenation-of-snow/flurry.

was it ever
mine to ur-command?
will it ever be?

arisen/to seek to find

To live it again is past all endeavor . . .
COLE PORTER

it could be
sex or
reincarnation —
a prodigal's return maybe?

it might be
spring or
any old yearn/
burning for one
more try or thing —
tra-lah/tra-lee. . .

it's all the same to me?
to love/to live & yes —
please —
as 2 bodies meet-hip-to-thigh
in that bolero rhythm —
we-do-begin-again — the beguine.

staccato/every which way repeats itself? (cosmogonica)

[gone/gone/again?]

the code decrypts:
stars loop
& signal back —
flint-y-
sem-semaphore/sparks
spark into fire
the first cause/effect
— a-bu-bursting conflagration/
irradiated light.

[a ghosting
burns upon the night-
side of
my retina/
my hallucinating eye.]

scintillant/in-scattershot:
i hear you call/
i reply —
pinwheeling&awe-constrained
&ooh-lah-presto?
(✳)
you/you . . .
re-vivify/are arisen.

[cymbals & ankle bells & myrrh.]

do your feet ache to touch the ground —
will you bide awhile?

cupid with day-of-the-dead necklace & star

Foolish

*h***O***pe* —

he **R***eturns*

— *be***G***s*

*one n***I***ght to*

*pro***V***e*

*tru***E** *— he lays*

the **M***oon*

*at my fe***E***t.*

math/at shut of day in 8 colors

(i)
she's
tricycling along
the rim of the known world when an
Orange-eyed-toad stops to chat . . .
3 in 1 —

divinity resides in a tetrahedron — don't you think?

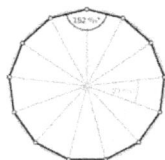 or a 13-gon?

(ii)
[nightjars
lay 1 or
2 cryptically patterned
eggs

directly onto bare ground]

ta-
trot/trot/ta-trot to
field center — circling to mark

a spot for treasure/box of
gaudy paste.

salt-y air — a trace of oil wells & Iodine waves
— but nightjars?

[in some other world . . .

small
feet of little use
for walking — long
pointed wings/plumage colored to
resemble Bark or
leaves.]

(iii)
at spooky distance now:

a 6-year-old cowgirl — 6-shooters/
Mercurochromed thumb/plastic-
fringed skirt/Turquoise
ankle boots —
moving

fast —
commandeers a field of cheatgrass/Mustard/thistle . . .

[nightjars/
1 girl —
an Orange-eyed toad —
spilling onto bare ground.
Mercury

now gone retrograde/Roan Blue.]

Mercurochromed sea-edge — rustle/coo — *shhhhh.*

0/marking time (rain rain go away)

after John Cage

ca-
cascading —
circadian/euclidian/non-
sensical:
sheets-of-water-oh-well.
what else could there ever be?
wah-what/&-whyever-not?
. . .
nothing-at-
all-to-do/to-say —
nothing-at-all.
no-nothing-at-all-
to-say/to-do
to-say-to-do-to-say —
to-do/to-say no-nothing-at-all.
. . .
opere citato.

elemental/locked in rock rock air

how to explain unless you invoke water . . .
ANONYMOUS

cosseted
in/wedded to
the mineral ringwoodite —
water
is wa-watering
as it will
(most of us
unaware of
such goings on) — co-
mingling
400 miles
beneath our feet/in-
sinuating
through the sedimentary
etcetera — earth's carapace.
siren/sum-summoning
water bodies
kind-to-kind —
us tidal creatures
— through its
particular thrum/sough . . .
to seep/weep (to bridge/bind) —
water seeks to find: wa-
water (ra as it rises).

& if you've missed the point — i'm saying
our bodies/terra conspire as water/wa-watering
seeks kind-to-kind —
to-bind.

. . . complete in the blink of an eye.

starlings in american elm/2

againS**t** my

Wishes

i dream**E**d

i f**E**ll

to**T**ally/

Recklessly in

lov**E** with

a fro**G** — i

d**R**eamed

h**E** was

fai**T**hless.

hoodwink/no kidding a kidder in 5 colors (a fable)

a trickster —
down on his luck —
visits 3 bears . . .

(let's call him *sid*).

a long way from his cold
home — he knocks at the door of
his boyhood friend . . .

(it's a 70° xmas in bell gardens/ca).

sid
is undoubtably
a bad man

(at the very least a con/a cheat).

almost
everyone knows this
except for

the friend —
though i'm 90% certain
he

knows but feels
a loyalty/an
empathy for the wily among us.

sid of course can dance —
so the friend's canny/Red-headed wife
makes a self-amused exception.

& their 8-year-old daughter —
well she simply likes him.

he has 1 eye/the
other made of glass: Sea Foam/
Amber variegated iris/a dot of Black.
sid gives her

her first bike —
a bit battered/
Tawny — with bejeweled

fenders/
a warning bell/
streamers flowing out from the ends

of the *new* handlebar.

she sees
the demon light
in his Tawny/proud eye
as she —

a-prideful-natural —
is bedazzled/riding away so demon fast.

axle/every which way (dervish)

i
tend to
go in several
directions at once.
in aerial view
the
starting
path looks
similar to spokes
coming
off the hub
of a wagon wheel/
like . . .
well — you
get the picture:
i radiate —
centrifugal flow —
flower + fluoresce?
to find
an effusion
of — i twirl/spin:

again —
i π & radius square.

the new world/31E

stalwart/no courage without conviction

there's
a weird beauty
that happens sometimes
when
under duress
pride and endurance kick in;

when
under onslaught
a determined arc of light
harnesses
much deeper steel —
abiding — purposeful intent;

when
on a particular day
an albatross scudding blueness —
                ghost-y light —
penetrates
(the brine-y-swell)
your b-bursting/striving heart

& your fortunate/truest self rounds
the unbidden divide.

Beauty
g**R**ace this
n**I**ght —
st**A**y.
p**R**omise me

sta**R**s
a g**O**ld ring
hi**S** bright
ey**E**s.

voir-dire/a point of faith in 5 colors

. . . and to your scattered bodies go.
JOHN DONNE/*DIVINE MEDITATIONS #7*

(i)
for a stretch in your 20's
you are so grief stricken/lost
you can't catch the city bus that
arrives at the corner every 15 minutes.
then one day —
sitting in a field/watching
the sun edge a small butte —
you bargain with God/the Spirits-That-Be
with whomever/whatever
is the source of those voices
you've heard for as long as you can recall:

ok —
if i'm not simply crazy
— hear me.
i don't know how to live
so if you're real/have some grand plan
then fine —
i'll listen — but i need
proof.

. . . so/0 . . .
weeds-rubbing-stems&tops-together.
after a bit you go back to
your friend's place — you're in transit/
living out of a battered footlocker
— and you fall asleep
        . . . dream of a dog:
mottled Black/White/Fawn &
tattered —
one Blue eye/one Brown with
a-lightning-streak-between-those-eyes —
bereft/forlorn
— pressed up against
the back wall of pen #19.
(#19)
& so the dog is:
wary — but there.

(ii)
being fanciful
you name the dog Lapis Lazuli —

(zuli-my-zuli)
— after the Yeats poem/the afghani stone/the one
Blue eye.
but when zuli is
full grown/a middle-aged girl —
a voice says:
the truth of it . . . 'the zuli'
is born out of the starry hem of Erzuli's skirt.

[*]
Erzuli:
the vodoun love goddess —
goddess of elemental forces/of beauty/
of dancing   flowers   jewels   &   pretty clothes.

(. . . a conjugation of nature/finery)

(iii)
15 years pass —
you move across the country/move
again/learn better how to live.
the zuli grows ancient —
warted/arthritic/rag-tag —
yet still insistently present/unaccountably

beautiful.
you know zuli is old
but her dying comes on fast
and you fear you're not
good enough/strong enough to let her go
— not enough grace or courage.

(zuli-my-zuli)

the night before she dies —
you are panicked/in-out of sleep when
— close to dawn —
a voice says:

there are 3 questions.
who are you? where are you? why are you?

& since you still don't believe
let me answer —
you are God/you are God/you are God.

is this proof enough?
surely out of the divine hem of/no doubt?
it's your choice . . .

a slow rise of color takes the room —
& barely audible — you hear yourself say:
yes   for this moment   yes.

so it's how/now (at last) — you bow to God?
how else do you come to be whoever it is
you are?

fame/rise fall of it (gertrude stein)

my pb-copy/
the selected writings
has yellowed — fallen apart:

to paraphrase —
nobody knows it
'til everybody knows

it?
ah/well —
little by little

my sacred emily
so clearly expressing
something — we

begin again:
rose-is-a-rose-is-a-rose
— ah/well . . . 'til it's not?

hush-a-bye/a-dö-dum-ditty

i'm
revamping my
most intimate *zeitgeist* —
my
notion of things —
yet again. no
chance of
much control —
do'you know how it is?

i'm
now thinking
at its most-plain
i'll
simply breathe/
attend — make way
for delight or idiocy
or whatever may . . .
too-ra-loo-ra-li-until-the-day-i-die?
no attempt to defend either truth or lie —
each lie is chaff/each truth a
      constancy:
where clarity/kindness reside;
where sorrow illuminates recompense;
where drift/dross accompany great beauty . . .
and awe and the littered rose remains a rose.

does hope still abide beneath the dark
as we sally back toward the light?

fall-down church & moon

dream-signals/at the fire-y gate

my home planet is undone by cataclysm. i am not certain of the root cause, but the planet no longer rotates, leaving it cold/dark on the one side and white-hot-beyond-life on the other. all of the remaining beings from the world are floating in a small clutch in space about a mile or two above the dark side of the planet which is no longer a coherent ball, but more like chunks of mountain and valley compressed into an enormous eroded fist — more asteroid than planet. where there should be stars, there is only cosmic dust and gas reflecting the errant sun — the word 'errant' is spelled out before me in script, sparkler-style. a collective keening has just begun when i am pulled into shifting dimensions by a force that is amplified by a kind of ululating that breaks down the walls of space/time as i go. a voice says,
"we're late to the party."

we materialize on a barren plateau in a numinous dimension where there is a vast army gathering. i am introduced to one of the lieutenants with "she is one of us." the lieutenant is part Aleut, her 8 sets of ears are half-funnel-eared-bat/half-human. without preamble the collective ululates into a high-pitched roar — the air shatters as the present burns away.

i am levitating up near the ceiling of an archaic/vaulted library — it appears to be carved out of the side of a mountain — i am not yet quite certain which book i have been sent to retrieve.

✳

*w*I*ld/*

W*ild*
*be***A***uty*
*e***N**-
T*angled* —

A

B*riar*
*f***U***ll of*
*thorn***S***/full of*
*t***H***orns*

*& h***O***ly/in-*
vi[o]late **F***lowers:*

Radiant/

*de***E**p-

Dreaming

/**R**edemptive

*gl***O**ry:

Secret

*m***E**

Safely away.

ariadne/dark dark shine

In Memory of George P. Elliott

she bathed every evening at 5.
she bathed in a room
whose only light came
from one window,
a west window.
the room held a tub —
long/old/footed —
and a mirror —
tall/old/footed.
both stood free from the walls,
both possessed the space
around them.
they held their own,
each a vector —
one horizontal/one vertical —
a testament
not only to their own,
but also to the room's magnitude.
they held their own, and
although the tub was reflected
in the mirror, they stood,
each to itself, alone,
until she entered each evening,
at 5.

(ii)
she enters naked, the color of dusk,
with a clock and a towel.
she sets the clock down next to
the tub facing the mirror;
drops the towel beside the clock,
obscuring the clock's face. she fills the
tub taking no notice of the mirror,
and steps into the tub, sits,
her legs the length of it, her back
against the end,
her neck cradled on the edge,
her head back, her eyes closed.
she and the tub are reflected
in the mirror,
each of the three is alone.

there is little sound.
perhaps the room settles
and the floor or the walls creak.
the clock's ticking is at times audible.
the water ripples or splashes.
on occasion she sighs.
there is little perceptible movement,
but when she sighs,

and then it is slight, a small parting
of her lips, a lift of her chest,
her nipples rising barely above
the water's horizon
and sinking once again
below it.

(iii)
it was this day she knew
that somewhere within her, pain,
the pain she had thought would
consume her, was still nesting.
it was the first thought that broke
what had been for an
undetermined period of time
an undisturbed gray.
it was known, but not felt, and with
this knowing without feeling, she
recognized her numbness.
she could not remember when it was
the numbness had begun to swathe
her senses in its soothing,
redeeming gauze.

she remembered it had begun

in her fingertips, at the soles
of her feet;
that at first she had feared she was
dying of indulgence, of the pain
she had taken so completely into herself.

she remembered, too, that her fear had not
outweighed the relief she felt as the
numbness moved like fire, like
the pain once had moved,
up, and across,
meeting at her heart.

the pain.
the sky, which had always been
the measure for her limits,
which had meant to her,
her freedom
as she had felt it limitless,
moved in on her until it appeared
to be against her face —
not blue as the sky
she had most loved, but gray,
gray and flat. she felt as if the sky
which had been her freedom/her hope,

which had yielded so many layers of
transparent wonder,
which had been her own special looking-glass
had been suffused with smoke,
and as its opacity increased,
it had blindfolded her.

she felt closed in a room so tiny
that she became increasingly afraid
she would die
for want of air and space.
with the persistence of this sense
of suffocation, out of boredom
with her hope that the sky would release
her, out of curiosity —
with the need to see if the room
was breathing
close upon her as she had begun
to imagine — she turned around
in the room and saw, and was
stunned by the room's meanness,
by its pitiful, undecorated walls.

she saw, yet there was
no source of light beyond

the impenetrable grayness
that was the walls, that weighed
palpably upon the air
of what little space there was
between these walls.
she forced herself to ask,
"what kind of antechamber is this?"

she searched the walls
with her eyes,
then frantically with the tips
of her fingers —
running them over rough
inch after inch of a surface
not like hewn rock, but more
like pitted concrete — a concrete
poured whole as there were no seams.
her suspicions confirmed,
she was paralyzed by terror of
entrapment.

after a time this passed
and was replaced with pain —
indiscriminate, insatiable pain.
it spread like fire in a tinderbox.

she began to wail.
she wailed and began to languish
in the wailing as if it alone
could penetrate the walls of the room.

when the walls did not dissolve
of the magnitude
of the suffering in her voice,
she began to throw her body
against those walls.
but the walls were less
susceptible to her blows
than her body.
the pain's life became manifest
in the bruises that spread over her body.
its life became her life:
the wail her song, the casting her
body against the walls
her accompaniment and dance,
the bruises her creation.

entranced
by the steady rhythm
of this life,
she began to tear at her hair

and beat her body.
at times, between motion
and sound, she would feel elated,
she would feel that she had found
her own special rite.

at other of these times,
she would feel that perhaps
she had sinned,
and she was performing
her own destruction
according to the nature
of her sin.
never was the sin revealed.

and at still other times,
she would relinquish herself
to being the victim of a battle of forces
of whose nature she was not fully aware.

her speculation,
the noise of her suffering
was, in time, interrupted by
a sensation at the tips of her fingers,
at the soles of her feet

that began to command
more and more of her attention.
this new sensation seemed
not to come,
as she had assumed the pain
had come,
from the room itself,
but from some other place,
some foreign source.

she searched the walls for evidence
of an exit. she was reassured
by the same seamlessness
that had at first caused her terror
and later set her wailing.

no longer wailing,
she was watching, listening,
attempting to discern the nature of
the sensation, this numbness — yes,
that was it, numbness — numbness
that was spreading
like the pain had spread,
like fire.

she was afraid.

had she had a choice?
perhaps her sin
had been indulgence in the pain,
in her giving up,
immersing her life in pain.
the pain had come
and it had taken her —
its will had become her will.

and now?
now this numbness
was her dying — she was
being punished for this sin,
or was it a sin she did not recognize,
or was she a victim?
perhaps it was not a punishment,
but a continuation of the sin itself.
a new sin?

as the numbness
firmed and hardened around
what she called her very being —
that being she located

geographically,
as if she were a territory,
in her heart —
these questions lost their meaning.

then she knew,
as she had not known before,
there was no sin —
she was not a victim,
but a part of those forces
she had felt — that she felt —
yet could not decipher.
she felt as if she were being
swaddled in a chrysalis.

she had seen the chrysalis
of the Luna Moth swinging heavily
from the dead tree whose skeleton
dominated the living trees
that clustered around it
on the hillside behind her house.
she had seen furry black caterpillars
spin themselves shut
on the twigs
of bushes, in the hollows

of tree stumps, under the eaves
of her house.

she had seen the eyes
of the Luna Moth
break from their brittled case.

she had also seen
that some of these tiny cases
were never broken from,
never lost their shapes;
that these, in time,
appeared like paper lanterns
left hanging far past the celebration
— ready to be crushed or simply
to fall to a fine dust.

the last thing
she remembered having felt
was a snapping
as if an old garment's last thread
had given way.

(iv)
the water cools —

the light leaving the room
moves up the mirror,
glancing her face, the tub's edge.

she opens her eyes,
turns to the window — the sun
is dropping below
the windowsill. she stands,
turns to the mirror and looks at
herself —
the light like her body
runs the mirror's length. she sees
the window behind framing
the tub and her body as the light
runs off the top of the mirror —
and she sees the windowsill go dark.

she steps from the tub, bends
and picks up the towel.
the clock's face is again reflected in
the mirror. she dries herself, drains
the tub. she folds the towel over
her arm, picks up the clock.
she leaves the room —
she is shining, the color of night.

& ALL is shining.

she sees
where the peccaries look for mud,
where night passes with puma and the fox
. . .

& ALL is shining.

[coda]
dark dark shine.
if she doesn't shine is she darkness?
i think not —
it's possible to hide a light —
possible to fall through
the beyond-black into a whole new life.
so here at the end it must be said
— who knows where a light
is inclined to shed:

as far/as deep as the eyes can see —
& ALL is shining.

[and love/and wild?]

ACKNOWLEDGMENTS

Some of these poems were first published in the following publications — some in earlier versions:
Annandale Dream Gazette ("dream-signals/at the fier-y gate"); *Mom Egg Review* ("fame/rise fall of it"); *MungBeing* ("1914/a few heartbeats before the war in 5 colors," "axle/ every which way (dervish)," "breach/Black ice in 1 color," "concupiscence/wisteria & elm," "topsy-turvy/thru the wormhole in 1 color," "dowsing/we find our way in 5 colors," "elemental/locked in rock rock air," "errant/by any other in 3 colors," "shadow-play/to cease to be in 2 colors," "vivify/ lift me up in 4 colors"); *Poetry Super Highway* ("hoodwink/ no kidding a kidder in 4 colors"); *Trickster* ("hoodwink/no kidding a kidder in 4 colors" in revised version).

My retrospective thanks to the late George P. Elliott whose conversation and encouragement meant a lot to me—his passionate love of literature and 'the good life,' however we may find it, pointed the way. My gratitude to the fine writer and artist, extraordinary friend, Holly Anderson (1955–2017), for her brilliant insight and generosity— her irreplaceable, ferocious soul. I am indebted to the poet Katrinka Moore for her last-minute read of the manuscript when my eyes/ears were blind/deaf. My appreciation to Mark Givens at Pelekinesis for his indefatigable support of writers of many stripes. The quotes from Heraclitus and Ibykos are thanks to the luminous translations of my friend, poet Brooks Haxton. And as always, I couldn't do without the good company of my family and friends.

www.ingramcontent.com/pod-product-compliance
Lightning Source LLC
LaVergne TN
LVHW041301080426
835510LV00009B/829